Foreword

As a believer I have experience blockage in hearing the Lord and receiving the word of the Lord. Hearing from God is crucial in our relationship with God. God speaks to us to give us divine direction and comfort
through the Holy Spirit. In any relationship communication is vital. Communication is a two-way street. Communication involves listening, speaking, and understanding. Clarity (of what is said) is a tool that causes communication to be successful.

How will our relationship benefit from knowing biblical and spiritual strategies on how to keep the lines of communication flowing? Throughout this book I will tell walk you through reasons why we as believers have issues with hearing the Lord and receiving the word of the Lord. I will give you Scripture to relay why God wants to speak to us and wants us to listen to Him. Nobody has all of the answers, but Him. Knowing that God has all of the answers satan, his imps, and the evil forces of this world wants us to stay bound. Having blocked ears prevent us from hearing from the Lord and knowing how to navigate in the spiritual realm effectively.

Preface

Being a millennial, I have not seen many books written by my age group on how to maneuver this thing named: SALVATION. I am no expert as I am working out my own soul salvation DAILY!!! I am, however an obedient servant of God out here working my post to save as many lost souls; redirect the ones that had hope and lost it; and to provide strength to those who are on the path, and to encourage those maybe weary in this season.

Choosing Freedom: I HAVE OPTIONS!

There's a breaking in the spirit there's a shifting in the spirit those lyrics really illustrates how life causes transitions. Transitions causes change. Change often includes new. With the new the old can't exist. The power of change! Yes, the power of change. Changing is the ability to exercise and create opportunity. Opportunity is the ability to accept, "I HAVE OPTIONS!" Yes, say that 7 times. It must be a complete statement in order for it to take hold into Your life. What would make it a complete statement? I'm glad You ask that question; You and I believing, "Opportunity is the ability to accept, I HAVE OPTIONS!" I can say that sentence with no conviction, no purpose, no expectations. And You know what'll happen by my saying that powerful statement without form, nothing! Nothing at all. You know why? Nothing from nothing leaves nothing, but that powerful statement spoken with convicted belief, purpose of intent, and expectation upon a beneficial return. Oh, now You're cooking with a recipe to stir up Your gift and to maximize Your life. I mean what is life except we get the most out of it.

The great exchange of the WORLD of man for the WORD of God. So, You and I are both today years old when we realized that it's only an "L" that differentiate those two words. My favorite advise to people is, don't get tricked by the trinkets of the enemy. He loves to imitate God. He roams the earth using the his limited demonic attacks with natural realm, the world, to deter people from being invested and living through the spiritual realm, the Word of God. What is it that God offers that the enemy can't? That's a loaded question. I know for me right now it is peace. Peace of mind. Peace of direction. Peace of understanding. Peace in knowing he will provide. Peace in knowing his omnipresence keeps my family. Someone else may say grace, mercy, second chances, healing, keeping power, financial assistance etc. Peace is the ultimate gift that I experience with God.

Open up Your heart and soul God will transform Your mind. Before You know it You'll have adopted the life of Christ, the beautiful life that he has predestined for You to have. There is no sin greater than his forgiveness. I bind the enemy from making You think that freedom from any of his bondage is a life sentence. In the Name of Jesus You are set free, healed, delivered, and moving forward in Faith AMEN.

Names of God

God has many names and many titles because he is everything to us. Calling Him the appropriate name according to what You and how You need Him to show up in Your situation is important in prayer and supplication. They are listed, so that You can add them to Your prayers and cries to the Lord.

Elohim- The very first name He was called in Genesis chapter one, it describes His position as the sovereign preeminent God.

Yahweh (Jehovah)- This name, which means Lord and Master, was used by the Jews but Jewish tradition considers it too holy to utter or write Yahweh, that they wrote it without the vowels so it would appear as YHWH. By the third century, Jews stopped using it altogether for fear of violating the fourth commandment of taking the Lord's name in vain.

Yeshua- Jesus' Hebrew Name
means salvation. It is only with this understanding that we can recognize Jesus' Hebrew name throughout the Old Testament. Jesus' disciples wouldn't have called Him anything other than Yeshua.

Yahweh Tsuri- is the Hebrew name for God, meaning the Lord is my rock

El Elyon- It means "The Most High God" in reference to His nature as the majestic ruler over all.

Adonai- This means Lord or Master, a name substituted by the Jews to Yahweh.

El Shaddai- El is related to Elohim and is used in conjunction with other words to describe God. Shaddai means to overpower. Putting them together would form the name Lord God Almighty to describe His nature as an all powerful God.

El Olam- Translated as Everlasting God from the word "Olam" which means everlasting.

El Roi- God sees me

Jehovah Jireh- Jehovah (used interchangeably with Yahweh) is the proper name while Jireh means "to provide." Putting them will form the name "God the Provider."

Jehovah Rapha- Rapha means heal so the two words translate to "the Lord Who Heals You" or "God the Healer" for brevity.

Jehovah Nissi- Nissi means flag which translates the name to "The Lord is My Banner."

El Qanna- Qanna means jealous, which speaks of His nature as a Jealous God who cannot stand other gods before Him as mentioned six times in the Bible.

Jehovah Mekoddishkem- The word Mekoddishkem means holy. If used together with Jehovah, it will form the name "the Lord Who Sanctifies You."

Jehovah Shalom- Shalom means peace thus, "the Lord is Peace" when connected with Jehovah. Modern Christians translate this these days as "Prince of Peace."

Jehovah Sabaoth- Used in conjunction with Jehovah, Sabaoth means the "Lord of Hosts."

Jehovah Raah- Raah means shepherd and when used together with Jehovah means "the Lord is My Shepherd."

Jehovah Tsidkenu- Tsidkenu means righteousness and will form the title "The Lord Who is Our Righteousness" if used together with Jehovah.

Jehovah Shammah- The word Shammah simply means there and if connected with Jehovah will translate to "The Lord is There."

Ruah- (pronounced in Hebrew Ruach), is the Hebrew word translated as God's Spirit. However, the word is also translated as breath, air, and wind in the Scriptures, reminding each of us of the physicalness of God's presence in the world.

El /Jehovah Gibbor- The Mighty God

El Gibbor- is a picture of God as a Warrior and Champion; gibbor means powerful, strong or mighty.

El Sali- God my rock God of my strength

Confusion of voices

The most interesting fact I learned about sheep is they are dumb. I learned this because someone who doesn't believe in the voice of God told me, well asked me rather why would God write that believers are like sheep and sheep are dumb? They can't think for themselves; are not the cleanest of animals; can't operate independently; life expectancy is 10-12 years and of those years they're only good for 5 years; are emotionally complex (like us); and they have no defense mechanisms which makes them targets for wolves. So, why then would God choose to align our nature to that of an animal that has many negatives about them? Because sheep are also submissive; stick together; pure in heart; not focused on their individual agendas, but rather the objective of the shepherd; don't waste the time given to them to accomplish their purpose; and they are social animals who have the ability to self-medicate (I did not know those facts https://spca.bc.ca/news/fun-facts-about-sheep/). Nonetheless sheep are about their business, following their Shepards commands, leadership, and protection. Is this not the way believers are to conduct ourselves as God is our Shepard? If we would spend our time replicating the obedience, selflessness, and mission focus nature of the sheep God invented this salvation walk would be better, not easier. We can't control the disappointments of life we had to face before accepting to be sheep, but we can control our attitudes after we accept the lifestyle as part of God's Holy Heard.

Knowing who our leader is will aid in us knowing who to listen to. To know God is to have time with Him. Spending intimate time -REGULARLY- with our leader will equip us with the familiarity of His voice. Knowing what a move of or intervention from God feels like. Knowing God does not suggest that we'll never be surprised by Him or something He does, but merely suggest that I will be more likely to know what is "Him" and what is not. Familiarity of His voice gives us the ability to identify people of His flock by their behavior. To know what His silence means. To readily differentiate imitations of God's. Lastly, to know the things, behaviors, and places He disapproves of. When we are in relationship with someone, we go to great lengths to learn them. Why? Our time, efforts, and money will be invested in this relationship, and we must know if this person is worthy of it all or is it a waste of time. What's different of the relationship we yearn to have with God? The relationship with God gives those things back to us, plus spiritual protection, healing, and the very air we breathe, He provides. Which should suggest we should go out of our way to solidify this relationship. We should center our lives around a God that does so much for us and need very little back. Right? Unfortunately, this is not the practice of believers all over the world which is why satan sits around waiting for us that have neglected prayer time; are disengaged from fellowship; have opted to self-reliance and not the leadership of the Holy

Spirit; and who are broken in any way. Satan is after every opportunity to deceive us that he imitates and wishes he is like God and he has fruitless benefits that will fulfill our emptiness. I read a passage in Luke 12 that made me understand why the brokenhearted are after possession and why greed is a symptom of the wrong path of life. The more we work to be fulfilled with the love of God the desire to have the lust of this world in our life fades away.

Hearing can be a deceitful situation. We can think we heard one thing and did not. We can audibly hear someone sitting right next to us talking, but because our focus is somewhere else, don't know one thing they said. This is also known as selective hearing. There are always other stimulants around us, people, animals, vehicles, machinery, electronics, water, structures, and just our own breathing can interfere with receiving a complete message. I'm sure none of us think about the auditory distractions or how to minimize them with every conversation with other people, more or less our conversations with God. I know for me I have often struggled with staying focus during prayer because an errand or task pops into me head and then boom my own voice is loud in my head as I make my petitions to God. What does that have to do with hearing from God? Hearing from God requires control over our minds. Disciplining our minds to stay still as we pray, while training our ears to know the voice of God is a hand in hand process. Easily we can think we heard God say something with all assurance and it was our own desires. Some will argue that this doesn't happen to "saints", but it does. Now, whether or not we admit our mistakes of saying that something was God is another topic, but it happens. It has happened to me. Simply because the voice of God comes to us in our spirit man; whereas our thoughts are within our minds and if we are without a filter, messages will be distorted. This is why just sitting and waiting on the voice of God is a very hard task to complete. The reality of the wait is that the wait will deliver a reward that will propel you and I into our purpose with divine accuracy.

The voice of God is a pristine quickening. Yes, He can be the Lion of Judah, roaring and demanding our attention. Often He is the Lamb of God, sweet, gentle, and waiting on our invitation. This is the reason why we can't have our spirits all muddled up with voices: the voice of naysayers; the voice of generational curses/consequences/witchcraft; the voice of unforgiveness; the voice of grief, pain, and anger; the voice of our parents and sphere of influence; the voice of doubt; and so many more.

John 10:27-30 KJV
"My sheep hear my voice, and I know them, and they follow me:
27 My sheep hear my voice, and I know them, and they follow
me: 28 And I give unto them eternal life; and they shall never
perish, neither shall any man pluck them out of my hand. 29 My
Father, which gave them me, is greater than all; and no man is
able to pluck them out of my Father's hand. 30 I and my Father
are one.

PRAYER:

Lord, I thank You. I thank You for how I know that I am Yours. I give You my best praise. Not because of how I feel or what I have, but simply because You are worthy. You're worthy of all the honor. You're worthy of all my time, energy, and effort. You're worthy of my submission. The way that I feel after understanding my shortcomings is not grievous, but enlightening. You did not let me die in my ignorance. You allowed me the latitude to see that there was a problem, identify the problem, get to the root of it, and address it with Biblical and spiritual guidance and Holy Ghost instruction and comfort. Forgive me Father for being in error of Your ways and living a life not led by Your voice, and Your voice alone. Forgive me for giving anything else the space that I now reserve for You. Lord let me apply what I have learnt about myself from now on. I don't have to wait until tomorrow to evict the voices that don't belong to You. I invite You in and serve notice to worry, fear, doubt, and any counsel that was not ordained by You to come into my life. I am Yours and You are mine. Allow me to be so spiritually sensitive that when anything mimics You, my discernment will immediately be on high alert and I will stop it at the gate. Stir up my desire to seek You deeper in the word; to be surrounded by revelation; and to dwell with believers who will empower me by their testimonies of how they waited and heard from You. I decree and declare that from this day forward You have all authority to speak freely and to occupy my spirit uninterrupted. In Jesus Name. Amen.

STATE OF ACTION:

Pray and ask God to cover your mind before each activity.

Sit quietly and pray for 3 minutes with a timer immediately after reading this. What did you hear?

Sit quietly and pray for 5 minutes each for 3 days with a timer. What did you hear?

Compare the list and determine why do you think your heard what and who you heard.

Define what invades your thoughts when God is speaking?

List the people you trust, things they say to comfort you, why this comforts you and whether their words propel or deter you from a posture of living in God's promise for your life.

How do you feel when God speaks to you?

Do you prefer the Lion or the Lamb and when do you need the opposite of what you prefer?

"Ok, I admit it"

There's a problem with my hearing? Right. A shocker. Hearing from God is a delicate tool. A tool that doesn't requires using the physical ears, but the ears of our spirit man. The spirit man requires hard work to build up, maintain, cause interruptions, and to restore. During the season of spirit man building or experiencing interruptions that still small voice-Lamb of God or the roaring declare-Lion of Judah can be distorted or even inaudible. In this moment patience is absolutely being tested and lack of patience couple with frustration can potentially place at the feet of desperation. Desperation creates illusions, we'd believe we heard God say something and it turned out to be something or someone else. Listening to illusive instructions and comforting words creates distractions from the path God wants us to stay on. That distraction can cause us to prolong a promise and lose faith. The best course of action to do when you are uncertain is to wait and ask God for a specific sign for confirmation. Often times God sends confirmation via prophets, preached word, meme's, build boards, license plates, strangers, little kids, etc. God will use what He wants to get the point across we just have to willingly wait on Him and listen intentionally.

We can choose to have selective hearing. Naturally we can be sensitive to certain words and phrases or words spoken by certain people like "babe, our name, mom or dad." Spiritually we have the luxury of knowing what His voice and tone specific sounds to listen for as His sheep. Our hearing from God can be great or poor it just depends on how loosely or secure we are taking our part in our relationship. It can't suddenly be gone or diminish over time go away. It is an progressive occurrence that can easily be overlooked. Rather it gets overlooked or noticed, it is a problem. A problem that needs our immediate attention. Problem's unaddressed don't go away because we ignore them. Problem's unaddressed often bring about more issues. More issues make it harder to find the source of the new problems. Which means that while we are fixing and exerting energy for the symptoms the original issue (root caused) is being unaddressed, buried, and dangerously becoming a part of your identity. Who wants to be known as the person who don't hear from God? Nobody.

How can we fix a hearing problem?

- Recognizing the problem is the first step in the process.
- Accepting that there is a problem. Well, isn't recognizing and accepting the same thing? Nope. You can see something is wrong and deny it's power of affecting your life which will keep you stagnant.
- Surrender your will to God. Surrender your ear gates, eye gates, and unbelief to God.
- Create more time to pray and study His word. When subtracting from the world we must add more of God.

- Identify the people, places, habits, and situations that causes hearing problems.
- Make a plan to change the problem. Set short- and long-term goals to measure your progress towards your plan.
- Identify accountability partners and prayer partners who will hold you accountable. This is key in any situation we need people that will root for us and pull on our coat tail aka Check us!
- Give yourself grace in the race. Go forth in greatness.

The Bible tells us countless times about how we should keep running. Keep going. No matter how many times we mess up. Keep going. If God can say ok, I see your sin and I raise you unconditional love, forgiveness, and peace; who are we to keep reminding ourselves or locking ourselves into that place of mistake, disobedience, or sin. Keep in mind I am speaking on true repentance where we strive change through the power of the Holy ghost, to do good, live righteous, seek the Lord, and find ourselves falling short. I am not speaking on living a lifestyle of disobedience or sin. God wants us to know He see's and He cares. Don't beat yourself up. James Chapter 1 let's us know that we will be tested. We will fall. We will learn and grow from our mistakes. God is always there. The word of the Lord will lead and guide us. And don't get caught up in religion and faking like you're holier than thou. Because none of us are spotless, our best is still like filthy rags.

Being renewed by the spirit is a daily and sometimes situations provoked occurrence. We have to be ready. We have to be equipped to let what we don't need in order to allow God to do what God does. We have to be conscience of our own fleshly desires. The enemy doesn't use the things that makes our neighbor weak he uses the things that we like. He uses things that make us compromise righteousness for fleshy satisfaction. Compromise starts off little. Well, I'll just skip this church or prayer event. I'll wear this on vacations only. I will turn up and drink on the special occasions. Forgiving them is a next year's problem. I will try again next week to read the word more. No, no, no, my love. As soon as we notice that we are compromising the character of God we need to stop, repent, and refocus. This is indeed how we find ourselves needing this book.

Understand the trick and devices of the enemy will ensure that we are equipped to fight. The tricks of the enemy masks themselves in many forms, but all come from lies, thievery, and an attempt to capture the believer's life and soul to damnation. He doesn't care about our money, health, family, or friends, but he will use whoever and whatever to get as close to us. Any crack in the door of our soul he's using it. We must keep our defenses up and recognize when we fall victim to any of the circumstances depicted in this book preventing us from not being able to hear from God.

Unforgiveness and Hurt

God is Almighty God. If we could just adopt the idea that He is mighty, has dominion, is omnipresent, merciful, just, and sovereign in the front of our mind we'll be cool. When somebody make us mad, and we are "sicking God" on them (like some yard Pitbull) hopefully we remember He's not some object to play with. But why can't we remember when our feelings are involved? When disappointment reached its last opportunity to strike in our lives? When restoration, healing, and peace in a relationship or situation seems impossible? God is still there. The enemy wants to obscure our vision and memory of how "He has never and will forsake (your name)." When he tricks us from being mindful of who God is and what He is capable of, that dirty slithering belly just laughs at our ignorance and gullible nature.

Unforgiveness and hurt takes time, but it all starts with misplaced hope. Yup, hope. We cannot have disappointment unless we first expected something in return or in conclusion of a promise given. There was a desire to give love before there was hate for a person, group of people, or situation. Before everybody in that family pissed us off, we had hoped in a family system. Before that boss stole credit for our work or denied our vacation time, we hoped in the system of honor, that we signed your name on. Before that relationship went down the drain we hoped for love everlasting, honesty, faithfulness, and safety. Before that child cut up in school, we hoped they would take the home training, love, and support we poured in them and presented themselves appropriately to the world. Before that church showed us that they are raggedy, we joined the church eagerly to be a part of a community, a body of believers. I could go on and on, but you think of one more opportunity to get you to a place of disappointment, unforgiveness, and hurt before ______________________________ I expected______________________________ ____________________. Now that I did not get what I expected am hurt and willing to work on

forgiving______________________________.

My forgiveness will require some true prayer, accepting my part in it even if I am simply guilty of allowing it to go on longer than it should have. We hear the statement, "forgiveness is for you." Well, it is so true. The person that wronged you has gone on about their next victim, I mean life. Why would you be required to stay stuck in time. It is neither a matter of forgiving nor forgetting. Forgetting the details, sequences of events, and resources shared during the time of time of trust before, during, and maybe even after the offense, YES FORGET ALL OF THAT. What you must not forget is your reason for forgiving them. A simple reason. I didn't think it was possible to simplify the betrayal, adultery, slander, heartache, and disappointed one did to me. After I healed and allowed God to put me in a posture of forgiveness I really he was simply ungrateful. That's all. Did those other things happen sure. Did they hurt? At the moment. Did I survive? You bet ya! Will he get another chance absolutely not.

However, he will get these prayers, forgiveness, and peace if I ever see him.
Forgiveness is a state of being, something we have to choose to do daily; with all situation, and people that do us wrong.

- Ezekiel 34:25-31 NIV

"'I will make a covenant of peace with them and rid the land of savage beasts so that they may live in the wilderness and sleep in the forests in safety. [26] I will make them and the places surrounding my hill a blessing. I will send down showers in season; there will be showers of blessing. [27] The trees will yield their fruit and the ground will yield its crops; the people will be secure in their land. They will know that I am the LORD, when I break the bars of their yoke and rescue them from the hands of those who enslaved them. [28] They will no longer be plundered by the nations, nor will wild animals devour them. They will live in safety, and no one will make them afraid. [29] I will provide for them a land renowned for its crops, and they will no longer be victims of famine in the land or bear the scorn of the nations. [30] Then they will know that I, the LORD their God, am with them and that they, the Israelites, are my people, declares the Sovereign LORD. [31] You are my sheep, the sheep of my pasture, and I am your God, declares the Sovereign LORD.'"

God takes care of His own. He will not allow anything or anyone to overtake us. He will not let the enemy to have triumph over us or anything that belongs to us. The issue is often times the battle may look lost or impossible to turn around and that's ok. "Improbable circumstances are God's breeding ground for miracles," a quote an old acquaintance has said to me on multiple occasions. As believers we quote that, "no weapon formed against me shall prosper!" Emphatically we declare this scripture when we believe victory is near. Then why don't we affirm it when defeat seems imminent? The Bible says that it won't prosper, but it will still form. The lies will be told. The theft will happen. The situation will rise against our victory, but the end result will be ordained victory by God. The results will not be what the enemy intended, that's how our victories are setup. Our test and trials are with purpose, for God to get the glory and for our faith to be increased.

Unforgiveness locks us in place. It locks us in that place of brokenness. It locks us in a place to not trust. It locks us in a place of not believing that

God is able to do exceedingly, abundantly. It locks us out of accessing all the blessings, promises, and goodness of God. It also locks us into a perspective that suggests that satan has the victory and we all know that that is a lie straight from his place of misery. I made a video years ago and I said, "being hurt and and mad at a person for something that happened any day or time before the present moment says that we are allowing that person who hurt us to still have control over us. Control over our attitudes, as soon as they walk in the room lips smacking attitudes up in flames and eyes are cutting. Allowing them to have control over our movements, if they are present, we don't want to be. Or we our going out of our way to be present to give opportunity for drama to pop off." Oh, it is so. Nobody outside of God and the person's name on the birth and death certificated assigned to us should have that much power over us.

Unforgiveness hinders our prayers. I remember on time I was terribly upset and was on a silent kick with my husband and honey my alarm for prayer went off. I hopped up to pray and the Lord said, so quick, "if you can't talk to him, don't talk to me." I'm like, but I want to talk to you, I do not have anything to say to him. I know I'm not alone with tantrums and silence. God does not care about what other's do to us that causes us to act ungodly or negative. We still must give an account for what we do in return. This lady said, "our response can determine the outcome of a promise." And if we believe that God will protect us as His sheep, His prophets, His anointed ones, and His children then we have to accept that He will take care of the situation and the people. WITHOUT OUR HELP!!!! I know I have tried to help Him on more than 100 occasions, but He got it down to a science how to handle the ones that afflict and hurt us. He knows what really would bring us all to our knees. He knows what is dear to our hearts. He allows things to happen because of our behavior, neglect for His word and His people, and for disobeying HIM. Some things that come to test us are for God to stretch us and to increase our faith. Whether

God created or allowed it to happen He is in control. Romans 8:28.

PRAYER:

Lord, You opened the heavens and gave the birds a song to sing and I thank You. You are beautiful and powerful in all of Your ways. I need you. I release all hurt and unforgiveness in my heart. I want to have a heart free from the things that would prevent my prayers from being answered. I want to be known as a pillar of peace and love. I want people who know my story to see that it was all You that changed my mind from holding onto unnecessary pain. I believe that You have purpose in the things You planned for my life, even the situations that I caused to happed Your word says You will turn them around for my good. I love how dedicated You are for my success and how sure You are that I can be healed and free from pain. I thank You dear Father for Your faithfulness. I praise You because I can always find You in my prayers. I continue to invite You into my life, into my home, into my family. Transform what needs to be transformed. Replace the words in my heart with words that spread grace to the offender and to myself. I ask all of this in order that You get the glory in the end. Prove to me that You are still a wonder working God and that my hurt is not too much for You to bare.

In Jesus precious name Amen.

STATE OF ACTION:

Write down the situation(s) and people you need to forgive.

Write down the losses you have had.

Write down how living with this hurt has affected you.

Pray over all the above items.

Revisit the paper in 10 days and see what has changed.

Continue to revisit it in 10 day spans to see how you are progressing. Eventually you'll get to a place of a light heart and will begin to protect it from ever returning to that place again.

Disobedience

So, our God in all of His infinite wisdom created us in His image. In that image He gave us a will, a desire to choose. We have a choice. I just love choices. Good choices like rather to buy 3 new shoes or 1new shoe, an outfit, and a new pair of earrings. I don't like to make choices when it has to do with making the right decision over what I want to do. Typically, that makes me feel bad because I don't get to have my way. I know I'm not alone. We all like choices until we can't have both things or all the options on the table. Even the will of God comes in 3 options His perfect, permissive, and acceptable will. To me and this is only what I think this is not the word of the Lord...I believe even when we make bad decisions, they eventually take us into a path of 1 of His appointed wills for our lives. We have all either seen the choose the red or blue pill meme on social media; have heard the scenarios of choosing door number 1,2, or 3; or watched the price is right. Choices takes us down paths that we will never even understand the "why" until we experience the results.

Having choices aren't a negative thing, it's picking the wrong choice that is negative. For every situation there is a bad and a good choice. I don't like when people say, "I'm in between a rock and a hard place." To me and this is just to me that means that both decisions are the same and will end the same and that is not true for any two choices. One choice is led by the Holy Spirit, covered in grace, and is God's perfect will. One choice is not the best-case scenario, but it will get the job done which I would suggest that this is His permissive will.

God permitted me to do things my way according to the knowledge and wisdom He gave us. One is the hardheaded choice half doing the will of God and doing what we want. This route that will hopefully prove to us that it is better for us to do things God's way, which is His acceptable will. It is not the way He intended for us to take, but it taught us some hard faith and life lessons. And then there is flat out disobedience which has none of the will of God in it, no desire to do things the Lord's way and its destination is not like any of the will of Gods'. Disobedience is a place that keeps us longer than we wanted to stay and takes us farther than we ever intended to travel. Disobedience is attractive. Why else could sin attract so many and is hard to abstain from. Bad things are tempting. Remember the devil does not present options that will not challenge our salvation, obedience, and faith. Temptation is the reason why mankind is in the predicament we are in now. Contrary to popular belief it was two people that made the CHOICE to disobey God, but only one person was given the instructions from God. That was Adam. The man, the first human, not the woman. This is not perspective it's factually based on the word. The word says:

Genesis 2:16-18 KJV

And the Lord God commanded the man, saying, Of every tree of the garden thou mayest freely eat: [17] But of the tree of the knowledge of good and evil, thou shalt not eat of it: for in the day that thou eatest thereof thou shalt surely die. [18] And the Lord God said, It is not good that the man should be alone; I will make him an help meet for him.

Now that you have read it for yourself, we see the chain of events clearly. God created the head of the household of Eden first and gave him specific instructions to follow. Those instructions were given before the woman was even on the scene, we can deduce that Adam told those instructions to the woman. Proof is in Genesis 3 where they begin the blame game and God checks Adam in verse 11 where He said, **"I commanded thee".** Thee is the same as YOU, so the translation of this section is, "don't blame her I told you not to eat it, you, Adam are responsible for your household."

A nasty spiral chain of events happened all because of disobedience to God, provoked by temptation of the enemy. Understand that the devil does not play fair. He knows what the ultimate reward of being in God's physical presence feels like. He knows the emotions of being overwhelmed by basking in God's glory and having no worries except to praise and rejoice in the Lord. The devil forfeited that reward with envy by thinking higher of himself and got booted from them pearly gates. Think of it like this if you had a really great house and had no obligations to keep it together, you didn't have to be financially responsible for the sustainability. Food is there at no cost. Bills are nonexistent. All you had to do was thank the owner of the home, keep the peace, obey the rule to stay out of the basement or you would lose the house and the benefits of the house. Then the person that use to live there came and said let's go in the basement. What would you do? Clearly, they understand what is at stake, misery loves company. This is not a fable the enemy is after our prize. He wants to add many to his camp by trickery. Don't let him trick us out of our peaceful eternity.

Disobedience is not a place that has safety in it at all. Disobedience forfeits the protection of God. With the exception of God honoring prayers of others. Disobedience walks in arrogance, with the disbelief that we know better for our life than the God that created us. The word tells us countless times about how God created us with purpose. He intentionally allows for us to be born.

There was no mistake in any of our conception. That alone is a weapon of deceit the devil uses to make us believe we have no purpose, to have us living with the mindset of unwantedness.

Deuteronomy 28 Genesis 19:26 AMP
But Lot's wife, from behind him, [foolishly, longingly] looked [back toward Sodom in an act of disobedience], and she became a pillar of salt.
1 Samuel 15:23 KJV
For rebellion is as the sin of witchcraft, and stubbornness is as iniquity and idolatry. Because thou hast rejected the word of the Lord, he hath also rejected thee from being king.

There is no reward for disobedience. When God gives directives there is no middle ground. He requires our complete obedience. Why? Every directive has blessings and rewards attached to them. He will not shortchange us on His word, so let's not shortchange Him on our obedience.

PRAYER:

Dear Heavenly Father, I come to You as humble as I know how. I glorify Your Holy name. Thank You for giving me a new day, a day I have never seen before. I thank You for keeping me from all harm seen and unseen. I am asking You to heal my heart. I need You to restore in me the desire to obey Your word and will for my life completely. Lord, it is You that have purposed and created me. I know that You have a way of escape for me to leave the life I am living for the life that has joy, hope, and peace all over it. Forgive me walking in disobedience and unbelief. Forgive me for being ungrateful of all that You have done, sacrificing Your only Son was just for me. I surrender to you today and open my life completely for you to have Your way uninterrupted. I bind the spirit of rejection right now. I am not what the enemy says that I am. I do not have to walk in darkness. I am not consumed by any witchcraft or generational curses that have my life as an assignment. Nothing will prevail over Your word of protection over my life. Not one of the enemy tactics no longer lay hold of my purpose. My promises will come forth and no longer will I walk in disobedience. I trust and believe that I will be great in Your name. I am a pillar of transformation.

In the mighty matchless name of Jesus the Christ. Amen

STATE OF ACTION:

Look up the definition for disobedience, rebellion, and purpose.

Write down the ways you have been disobedient.

Accept your disobedience with no shame!

Repent for your disobedience.

Daily pray for obedience and awareness of the enemy tricks, schemes, and pythons.

Pick one thing that you have been disobedient about and make a plan of obedience with a time frame to complete it.

After that time evaluate your growth and repeat until all the items are completed.

Always give yourself grace for the race. You will fail and make mistakes or get to busy to keep up with the process, but keep going!

Be comfortable to call yourself out for disobedience going forward.

Lack of faith

Hebrews 11:1 says Faith is substance of things Hoped for. Hope! Such a short word, yet so powerful. But how to have hope in a world where evil seems triumphant? Hope is built from watching God turn impossible situations into miracles time after time again. Hope is saying I don't even know what's going to happen, but I believe in the best possible outcome in Christ Jesus. Hope is bought with grief, pain, brokenness, sadness, lost, frustration, poverty, anger, stress, illness, and so much more. Hope is not cheap. To believe in something we can't see coming together or have enough resources to make happen on our own is an incredible gift. This gift is so incredible the devil is always after our hope. He has demons assigned to damage our hope. That is part of why I am a professed HOPE DEALER, however I can encourage or distribute hope I'm doing it.

I remember a time where fear had my hope wrapped up terribly and I was afraid to hope for anything. I moved and was afraid to move all my things in. New relationships I was on pins and needles thinking something was bound to go wrong. Family, I was under a certain notion that it'll always be the same, nothing will ever change. I was attending a church and waiting for them to be unwelcoming. Then the Lord told me, "get your hope up!" We cannot have faith without hope. And without faith we cannot acquire God's pleasure.

Having faith, building faith, or even losing faith happens over time. There are instances where people say losing such and such caused me to lose my faith or when this or that happened to me I lost my faith. Well, if one event shakes our faith then that means that it was on shaky and feeble foundation from the jump. Anything not built on the sure and sturdy foundation of The Lord God Almighty is destined to collapse. What people don't understand is that faith is a muscle. We must work it out daily or as much as we think we need faith. I have never had a situation make an announcement that it was about to require faith to get me through it. Or to let me know how much faith this event would require. Which means we must work on it and keep our faith buckets full or not on empty. We need faith just to leave out of the house. Faith to trust in God and not on what we see or what we feel. Faith to be the representation of faith while God gets the glory.

If my hope and faith are damaged, I will have doubt in everything. Doubt is the symptom of a lack of faith which causes us not to trust ourselves, God, other people, and surely not Holy Spirit. Doubt will have us questioning simple things that we know are true, like if we can accomplish something we have done all our lives. Not believing in people that have proven their loyalty to us. Not believing the Word of God. This is the danger of not recognizing that test and trials come to increase our faith. To make our faith stronger. To give us more reasons to trust God and to trust in God. We must combat the devil on all fronts and see him as he approaches us. In order to see the devil and to identify his tactics it requires the scales from drinking the deceit of the enemy to fall off.

Acts 9:1,3-5,18 AMP
Now Saul, still breathing threats and murder against the disciples of the Lord [and relentless in his search for believers], went to the high priest, [3] As he traveled he approached Damascus, and suddenly a light from heaven flashed around him [displaying the glory and majesty of Christ]; [4] and he fell to the ground and heard a voice [from heaven] saying to him, "Saul, Saul, why are you persecuting and oppressing Me?" [5] And Saul said, "Who are You, Lord?" And He answered, "I am Jesus whom you are persecuting, [18] Immediately something like scales fell from Saul's eyes, and he regained his sight. Then he got up and was baptized;

Trust in the Lord with all of our hearts (Proverbs 3:5) to disengage from doubt and to show the devil that none of our faith is not up for grabs. Let the storms of life come and do their job, which is to help build the people of God up, not destroy it.

John 10:26 KJV
But ye believe not, because ye are not of my sheep, as I said unto you.

Having faith and belief in God is a notable characteristic of those who belong to Him. To know Him is to trust Him. Trust in His track record, trusting in His unfailing Word. We must tailor our lives to always be a reflection of the God we serve. It will take time to go from a place of having a lack of faith in God to an abundance of trust in Him and His abilities. As always give (your name) Grace in this race. It took time to damage or destroy the faith we had, even if you never believed in God you believed in something or someone and it took time for that to happen. You got this!

Faith is an activity that can be done with others. Salvation in the end is a personal walk, but we can have greater success with this race running alongside others who will share in similar experiences, triumphs, and defeats. This world runs on testimony and awareness. Sharing my testimony helps me know that God is able to do exceedingly. I have lived a lukewarm life and seen how many times the enemy attempted to have me incarcerated, at odds with everyone, bullets flying over my head through my hair, and so many other interesting events that would have been prevented had I obeyed and stayed true to salvation. Look at me now and look at you now!

PRAYER:

Almighty God, Prince of Peace I worship Your presence in the earth today. I reverence You as Lord and Savior of my life. I declare that my heart is full from all of Your amazing power. I thank You for allowing breath to enter in my body and for my limbs to operate as You saw fit on this day. I thank You for the family and support I have in my life. I thank You for the test and trials I have experienced. The ones I have past, the ones that I have failed, and have learned from. I count it all joy that You saw fit to allow Your living word to come pass my ears and settle in my heart. I am not a perfect faith example, but I strive to be better. I strive to allow every area of my life to give You glory. I ask the You show me how to allow my faith to glorify Your name. I know that You have sent the Holy Spirit to lead and guide me. I open up my life for Him to direct me and to protect me from my unbelief. Amen

STATE OF ACTION:

Write down the areas that you don't have faith in.

Write down the reasons you've never exercised or lost faith in those areas.

Pray for understanding of faith.

Ask 3 people from 3 different backgrounds what faith means to them.

Make sticky notes of claiming faith some examples or options to use: I am a faith walker; I have faith in God; faith does not worry; I have faith that _____ will change; my faith grows each day; I give grace to myself while I learn in faith; MY(loud) faith WILL(loudly) move mountains; I put on faith before I take on the world; I have faith that God sustains/keeps me; faith walks with me in every test; my faith is not a secret; and I have mustard seed growth (understand the story before writing this one). Place them on the back of the front door, on all mirrors, fridge, and a few more doors.

Choose a faith ancestor in the Bible to research about.

Determine what one thing made them trust in God.

Determine the adversities of that ancestor.

How did they handle each situation carnality, spiritually, emotionally, and mentally?

Can you relate yourself?

Write down the research you know about yourself.

Determine what one thing made you trust in God.

Determine the adversities you've had.

How did you handle each situation carnality, spiritually, emotionally, and mentally?

Peace in mind

Peace is the most expensive attribute in our lives. There's not a circumstance or issues that peace can't help arriving to the solution or "IS" the solution to. I dare you to challenge that philosophy. Drama succumbs to peace. Hurt, inadequacy, anger, and all other negative emotions and attitude can't survive in a peaceful environment. Complex decisions need peace to segue a moment of clarity. I mean peace is the breeding ground for the presence of God to dwell. Yes, He can come in the midst of a chaotic situation, BUT when HE gets there, there is an atmospheric shift into a calm and security which creates PEACE. Glory to God! Peace is needed in us to hear the voice of our Father expeditiously. If peace was optional and dispensable why would the enemy work ever so hard to keep us from it? God is peace. His presence brings peace. We thrive in peace. Even Jesus understood that the command of Peace will restore hope and rebuke fear. What is robbing you of your peace? That is a loaded question. One could answer family, but is it family or the lack of support. Money. Is it money or the mismanagement of resources. Relationship status. I hate to bust this bubble. Love and security is an inside job. A person or the lack thereof should have no bearing on our peace. We ought to stop giving people authority over our lives that will shift, shape, or destroy our existence. God has authority that He deserves, and we just give it away to whatever and whoever makes us "feel" like they deserve the opportunity or same level authority as we give to Him. This is why our spirits are compromised with other people, things, and thoughts, because the response in our spirits that was created to respond to God is shared with idols. Idols are anything that you put before God or in His place/position.

What people fail to realize is that it is important to protect the eye gates and ear gates. Allowing unfiltered information or images in will cause a plague in our minds. The things we hear and see can deter us from living in a place of peace, becoming accustom to having moments of peace. If we infuse our eyes with reality tv; inappropriate/ungodly literature, social media, internet, and secular comedy, we must assume at some point those intakes will need a place to live and eventually regurgitate from. That place is our minds. We intake so much and our mind is sometimes overloaded with thoughts that it begins to misplace information and begin to have misfiring when communicating from one function to another. I'll prove it. You ever been in a position of stress just no assistance, no relief, little to no sleep, and then someone comes to ask you a question and you bite their head off (or get yours bit off)? The whole time that person was just going to offer assistance and be relief and an opportunity to just breath. That is a classic example of a misfire of information. Under normal circumstances we could have read posture and the cadence of their voice to know that their intention was never to add one more thing onto our plate, but to give another plate to help manage our plate or to altogether take some onto their plate and be the relief we need. Information overload is so easy when we are intaking information that should be given to God. I used to tell people that such and such is not my business it belongs to God (I wonder why I started back minding **His** business). Having a posture of "everything in my life is filtered through God" saved me much trouble, stress, misfires, and muffled messaged from God.

It is our responsibility to provide God a space not cluttered with the cares of this world in which we can't do anything about it except pray on it. Even if we start meddling and trying to fix things at some point we go to the Master because He makes all things new, fixed, and peaceful.

John 10:14 KJV

I am the good shepherd, and know my sheep, and am known of mine.

God takes care of His.

PRAYER:

Jehovah almighty. The Great I am. I love You. I praise You and I adore You. This world has dealt me some crazy and sometimes ugly cards and before I knew it, I'm depending on my own strength and not Yours. I am weak and useless without Your presence. Enter in and have Your way. Enter in and clear out the clutter, help me to make choices that will perpetuate peace in my mind. Help me to reject the identity of this world and assume the identity of Christ. Lord, teach me how be a pursuer of peace. Teach me how to draw towards peace and not live in fear thinking that all situations will end up in drama and or trauma. I lift my head knowing that it will no longer be weighed down with idleness and idolatry. Nothing comes before You. Give me the strength to address the situations, information, and relationships that can't stand in Your presence. They no longer has access to my eyes, access to my ears, access to my mind, and access to my body. I am Yours and you are mine. I declare. I will adopt the acceptance of ownership and not treat You as a second-class god and not believe the enemy when he tells me that I am not important to You. I invite the Holy Spirit in to navigate in areas where I am weak to protect me from my own fleshy desires. Forgive me for not operating as a man/woman of God. Forgive me for listening to and watching anything believing that my life belongs to myself and not to the Savior of my soul. I honor everything about You. I honor the mind that You gave me and give it back to You. Lord, create in me a clean heart and renew a right spirit in me. Oh Lord my strength and my redeemer. In Jesus name. Amen.

STATE OF ACTION:

Fast for 7 days without tv, social media, or anything that is not scripture or devotionals.

Fast for 7 days without listening to anything that is not a sermon or worship music, not praise.

Fast for 5 days without both.

How did each fast go?

Pray at the end of each day for a better tomorrow with this new identity in Christ.

What new habits did you develop to occupy your time?

Can those habits sustain you into a new way of life?

How did reading the word differ from before?

Has your desire to serve the Lord changed?

List the things that cause/caused your distraction

List the ways you address your distraction

Focus on one distraction at a time until you have gotten to a place of comfort in your mind without chaos. It's ok if you revisit or get stuck on a distraction.

Strength to submit

You must fight to find the sheep in you. Remember earlier on we talked about the characteristics of sheep in "ok, I admit." Access the faith assigned to you. Learn how to forgive, move on, and protect yourself by allowing God to be the vengeance in your life. We don't have much time on this earth, even if we live to be 130 years old. The biblical people were living centuries and God is eternal and none of us have that much time to keep getting it wrong, then right. Submitting gets tough at times. One compromise seems innocent until it's layered with more unrighteousness that puts us at risk of the wrong lifestyle. I mean like backsliding wrong, living in the state of disobedience, or not accepting God in our life from the jump before we take our last breath type of wrong. Don't let any false prophet or someone who can't or won't rightly divide the word for their own pleasure trick you that you can accept the Lord and live any kind of way. For what cause would we need salvation if living identical to the world is the standard? Be set apart for Heaven sake.

Proverbs 14:12,14,16 KJV
There is a way which seemeth right unto a man, but the end
thereof are the ways of death. [14] The backslider in heart shall
be filled with his own ways: and a good man shall be satisfied
from himself. [16] A wise man feareth, and departeth from evil:
but the fool rageth, and is confident.

Jeremiah 2:19 KJV
Thine own wickedness shall correct thee, and thy backslidings shall reprove thee: know therefore and see that it is an evil thing and bitter, that thou hast forsaken the LORD thy God, and that my fear is not in thee, saith the Lord GOD of hosts.

Romans 8:1-2,4-7 KJV
There is therefore now no condemnation to them which are in
Christ Jesus, who walk not after the flesh, but after the Spirit. [2]
For the law of the Spirit of life in Christ Jesus hath made me free
from the law of sin and death. [4] That the righteousness of the

law might be fulfilled in us, who walk not after the flesh, but after the Spirit. [5] For they that are after the flesh do mind the things of the flesh; but they that are after the Spirit the things of the Spirit. [6] For to be carnally minded is death; but to be spiritually minded is life and peace. [7] Because the carnal mind is enmity against God: for it is not subject to the law of God, neither indeed can be.

With the little time we have we must learn to operate in a way that pleases God and tells the devil to "get the steppin'." Even in tough times it is imperative that we stick with the Lord, unite with our fellow faith walkers, have fun, trust God, and meet up in Heaven, because the alternative is wack and I heard very hot.
I wrote this book using a lot of we and I didn't even know until I got to the part about sheep and the Holy Spirit let me know we can't do this alone. None of us can successfully accept the call to live for a God we can't see. Change the world around us, by being the change we want to see provoked in the world. Feel as if we are being ate up and spat out sometimes daily, by the very system we are working tirelessly to change. Have a marriage and raise a family in this

world and around other believers. We can't do it without the word of others testimony and without allowing those testimonies to encourage our walk. To give our salvation fight more knockouts with unified praying and fasting. With the gathering of saints, no matter how many churches and bodies of assemblies there are for the cause of God through Jesus the Christ, we need them all. I need you and you need me. That is the unadulterated truth about life. Which is why the enemy works tirelessly to wreak havoc amongst the saints. Why he is always using that little bit of pride and unbelief to create false witnesses and corrupt teachers to spread his cause. The enemy is always working, BUT SO IS GOD. God never sleeps nor take naps; it does not say that about the enemy. God is the only omnipresence, the enemy sends his imps and work overtime to gain what we think are victories for him, but remember **ALL THINGS WORK TOGETHER FOR GOOD (not for the good) FOR GOOD-Romans 8:28.** It is so that the things that the devil plans, fails and aid in the agenda of God in God's people. The sooner we adopt and stick with this ideology the sooner we can stop giving credit where credit is not due.

We are stronger in numbers. We thrive as a body to bring about change, effective change and growth. It is the body of believers that has held this nation together. It is a body of believers that declared that segregation and blatant racism cease. It is a body of believers that has stood up for government change and no matter how we think it will never change, stop that thought and look at the progress that this country has taken. I am absolutely against and for everything that God stands for and is against unwaveringly; however the one thing we all seem to forget while standing with God is to have and show the love that He carries. Love doesn't hurt. Love does not separate/segregate even by forming or joining cliques. Love does not look down and refuse to help. Love does not boast and brag on accomplishments that were only possible by the allowance of the greatest Trinity I know: God, Jesus, and the Holy Ghost. Love shows up and is ready to help. Love brings peace. Love unites. Love is not ignorant. Love has grace. Love sets boundaries. Love lifts and holds accountable. Love honey is the greatest and most powerful emotion. Love often goes against what is logical or even legal to help the one receiving the love and love efforts. Love makes you do the unthinkable, to be the unchained and make a stand that, "I ____(your name)____ am the called of the Lord. I am not consumed by the ills of life. I have purpose and promise over my life and my family will be protected as I walk out my calling. I trust in God with all my heart, mind, body, and spirit. I submit daily to the things of God, for God, with the endorsement of the Holy Ghost."

Love will have you talking sweet somethings to the God that woke us up and while so many others didn't get the call. The love of God for God will have us changing in ways we just never thought possible. I know I get giggly and tickled thinking about how much God loves me, me, me, and me. Like for real I be doing the most, honey I tell my folks I know my guardian angles have retired young; cringe at the fact they're on my heavenly detail, and don't listen to them or do the polar-opposite of right because I am yet still a sheep that needs to grow (sometimes the hard way).

The results is not compared submission to a spouse or job that will eventually do something(s) to hurt us and sometimes cause us to leave. There is protection in submitting to God. He protects those that follow Him. He will allow the enemy to touch certain parts of our lives in order to show us how strong we really are. That's deep right? Right. Sometimes submission hurt and that's being real. Sometimes submitting feels like we're stupid because it seems as if the ones who say forget God and all of His glory are moving ahead, thriving, living their "best life", and doing better than us. In that simpleminded thought we know that God leaves no sin unanswered, no disobedience un-responded to, and certainly those who don't change in servitude away from Him will surely not enter Heaven. Believe that. I don't know about them, but I know that we over here are trying to make it in. Submission is not for the weak. We must make up our mind that this is what I am doing no matter what it looks or feels like, no matter the lost.

James 4:6-8 KJV
But he giveth more grace.·Wherefore he saith, God resisteth the proud, but giveth grace unto the humble. [7] Submit yourselves therefore to God. Resist the devil, and he will flee from you. [8] Draw nigh to God, and he will draw nigh to you. Cleanse your hands, ye sinners; and purify your hearts, ye double minded.

Submission is not a sign that we are weak, but rather highlights our strength to follow. I know you have heard it said some kind of way, "that a great leader must be a great follower." As a believer we are to be the greatest of followers. God trust us with so much. The responsibility to accept His love and salvation; change; and then be a beacon of hope is a tall order. Yes, we are to witness with our lips, but the greatest testimony we can ever have been, is our walk, our witness. It's one thing for me to say have love, be patient, and give yourself grace, but it's a better thing for people to see that I'm kind in the grocery store, I love on my family, I don't mentally beat myself up, and I give my time to ministry. We need to understand it is more important to be the witness we want people to experience, then do themselves. Rather than talk with a double tongue. It sucks to have powerful people who can talk a great game and then their entire walk comes into question when what they say and what they do just doesn't add up. I'm not talking about a simple uh-oh, I'm talking major contradiction to everything they stand on. I'm not giving no examples because we all fall short, but I'm sure you can think and probably are thinking about somebody as you read. We have to show the world there is reward in submission. There is reward in being the church. There is favor attach to the assignments of Christ and we can't reap the benefits unless we sow the humility of submitting to the greatest leader. A leader that has a track record like no other. A leader that sent His only and beloved Son to experience what we experience in this flesh and overcame death, so that we may have a chance to eternal life. A leader that will leave the 99 and go after that 1 lost soul. King of Kings and Lord of Lords, He opened crossed seas, He gave us the

Underground Railroad, He protected us from slavery, rape, the residuals of trauma, debt, suicide, so much more, and lifted our heads. He is the one and Only God our Father who sits on a throne worthy to receive our worship, submission, praise, honor, glory, and gratitude.

PRAYER:

Great God and Mighty ruler, I worship You with all of my being. I adore the air I breath because You make it possible. Lord, I thank You for allowing me to fight through the rough times in life even through the interruptions to finish this book. I know that there is strength in everything that has happened to me, around me, and because of me. I pray that in all You get the glory out of my life. Get the glory out of my transformation and walk. Get the glory out of my forgiveness of others and myself. Get the glory out of my testimonies. Get the glory out of submission to Your will and way for my life. Lord, remind me that my submission to You is not an act or scene, but a way of life. I live submission, I yearn for more submission, and I breath submission to Your will,

Your way, and Your desires for my life. I ask that from now on I have the mind to filter my desires and choices through You. I accept every protective block that the Holy Spirit creates to keep me from a hard lesson. I glorify Your name because You are gentle with me, You have had patience in ways I could never understand, and yet You still love and trust me to carry on the legacy that You are the Great I Am. Forgive me for every time I didn't understand or believe that You were. Forgive me for the life choices I made against Your will. Forgive me for not walking as I spoke and read in Your Word. Lord, I thank You for sparing my life up until this point. I praise You and lift You up. Save those around me who will watch my transformation and know that it was nobody, but You. Encourage my soul to keep the faith. Show me how to submit in a Holy manner. Keep me in all of my ways and let not my enemies triumph over me. I bless You always. King of Kings and Lord of Lords. In Jesus Mighty Name. AMEN

STATE OF ACTION:

Define what submission is to you.

Look up submission in the dictionary.

List the similarities and difference of definitions.

Pray for God tol tell you the ways He desires your submission.

Write 5 times you've experience submission whether being submission or receiving submission.

Look for 3 encouraging submission scriptures.

Set 3 alarms in your phone to go off daily for 21 days with those 3 scriptures.

Pray that God opens up the places in your life that you have not submitted to Him.

Write down the ways you are not submissive to God.

Re-visit the list in 10 days has there been any change even tho little things matter?

Re-visit the list in 30 days, is there something new you discovered that should've been on the list?

Ask someone you trust how do they think you are submissive and stubborn?

Ask God if He can use those behaviors?
Take yourself out on a date to celebrate your submission success

SUBMISSION is a lifestyle which means it takes time to craft not perfect, give yourself grace in this race love

www.ingramcontent.com/pod-product-compliance
Lightning Source LLC
LaVergne TN
LVHW091122150826
845673LV00002B/933